Engaging Your Audience:

A Guide to Building Online Communities and Utilizing Micro-Influencers for Business Growth in Online Marketing

Chris Kirton

Table of Contents

Introduction:

In the vast expanse of the digital landscape, where screens flicker and notifications never sleep, the heartbeat of business success lies in one simple yet profound concept: connection. No longer can businesses afford to speak to their audiences. The age of one-way marketing is over. Today, success is measured by the relationships you build, the stories you tell, and the communities you inspire. This book is your guide to mastering the art of engagement, harnessing the power of online communities, and leveraging the influence of micro-influencers to propel your business into new dimensions of growth.

The Shift from Broadcast to Conversation

Once upon a time, marketing was a monologue—a loud, unwavering voice that declared its message to the masses. But as technology evolved, so did human behavior. The modern consumer is no longer a passive listener; they are an active participant. They expect to be heard, valued, and involved. Platforms like social media have given them the power to engage, question, and even shape the brands they support.

For businesses, this shift is both a challenge and an opportunity. It demands authenticity, adaptability, and a willingness to embrace vulnerability. But those who master the art of conversation find themselves rewarded with something far more valuable than a one-time sale: loyalty. And loyalty, as we'll explore, is the cornerstone of sustainable business growth.

Why Communities Matter

At the heart of this engagement revolution lies the concept of online communities—spaces where people come together around shared interests, values, and goals. These communities are not just digital meeting places; they are ecosystems of trust and influence. A well-nurtured community can transform customers into advocates and advocates into evangelists.

Take a moment to consider this: Would you rather invest in a brand that shouts into the void, or one that listens, responds, and creates a sense of belonging? The answer is clear. Communities humanize businesses, bridging the gap between brand and consumer. They offer a platform for dialogue, collaboration, and innovation. In this book, we'll delve into the strategies for building, growing, and sustaining these vital networks.

The Power of the Micro-Influencer

In tandem with online communities, micro-influencers have emerged as the unsung heroes of modern marketing. Unlike their celebrity counterparts, these influencers thrive in niches. They may not boast millions of followers, but their audiences are fiercely loyal, deeply engaged, and highly targeted. Micro-influencers excel at building trust, and in a world inundated with advertisements, trust is currency.

Throughout this book, you'll learn how to identify the right micro-influencers for your brand, forge meaningful partnerships, and create campaigns that resonate authentically. Their voices, combined with the collective power of your community, can amplify your message in ways that traditional advertising simply cannot achieve.

A New Era of Marketing

This is not just another marketing book; it is a roadmap for those ready to embrace a new era. It's about understanding that engagement is not a tactic—it's a mindset. It's about shifting from transactions to relationships, from selling to storytelling, and from advertising to advocacy.

By the end of this journey, you will be equipped with the tools, strategies, and inspiration to not just survive but thrive in this dynamic digital landscape. Together, we'll unlock the secrets to engaging your audience and turning them into your most powerful allies. Welcome to the future of marketing. Let's begin.

Chapter 1: The Foundations of Online Engagement

Understanding Your Audience: The Key to Connection

Every meaningful relationship begins with understanding, and in the digital realm, the connection between a brand and its audience is no exception. Your audience is not a monolithic entity; it is a tapestry of individuals with unique needs, desires, and pain points. To engage them effectively, you must first know them intimately.

Imagine stepping into a crowded room, and trying to strike up a conversation without knowing who you're speaking to or what they care about. The result is likely awkward and unproductive. Now, imagine entering that same room armed with knowledge about your audience's preferences, struggles, and aspirations. Suddenly, the dialogue transforms into something genuine and impactful.

Building this understanding begins with data—demographics, behavior patterns, and preferences—but it doesn't end there. It requires empathy, listening, and a willingness to adapt. The most successful brands don't just collect data; they use it to craft messages that resonate on a personal level. When your audience feels seen and heard, engagement becomes effortless.

The Psychology of Engagement: What Drives Interaction?

Engagement is not a random act; it is deeply rooted in psychology. People are wired to respond to certain triggers—curiosity, validation, and a sense of belonging, to name a few. These drivers are the building blocks of online interaction.

Consider curiosity, the spark that drives us to explore the unknown. When brands create content that intrigues and invites discovery, they tap into this powerful motivator. Headlines that pose questions or content that promises solutions ignite a desire to learn more.

Validation is another cornerstone of engagement. People gravitate toward brands that affirm their values, preferences, or experiences. Whether through personalized recommendations or content that speaks to shared struggles, validation fosters trust and loyalty.

Above all, the need for belonging shapes online engagement. Communities thrive because they offer a space where individuals feel connected to something larger than themselves. Brands that cultivate inclusivity and foster genuine connections create an environment where engagement flourishes.

Crafting Your Brand's Voice: Authenticity Over Perfection

In the crowded marketplace of ideas, your brand's voice is its calling card. It is the personality that sets you apart and defines how your audience perceives you. But here's the catch: today's consumers crave authenticity over perfection. They don't want a polished monologue; they want a genuine conversation.

Think of your brand's voice as a human one. It should be warm, relatable, and consistent across all touchpoints. If your audience sees your brand as a friend rather than a faceless entity, they are far more likely to engage.

Take a moment to consider the brands you admire. Chances are, they have mastered the art of speaking authentically. They own their mistakes, celebrate their victories with humility, and engage their audience with humor and heart. Authenticity builds trust, and trust is the currency of engagement.

Choosing the Right Platforms: Where Engagement Thrives

Not all platforms are created equal. Each digital space has its own culture, language, and rhythm. Understanding where your audience spends their time and tailoring your approach to each platform is crucial for effective engagement.

For visually-driven audiences, platforms like Instagram or TikTok offer rich opportunities for storytelling through images and videos. For in-depth conversations, LinkedIn or Twitter might be more appropriate. The key is to meet your audience where they are and deliver content that feels native to the platform.

When you align your strategy with the unique characteristics of each platform, you position yourself to create authentic, meaningful connections. Engagement isn't just about showing up; it's about showing up in the right place, at the right time, with the right message.

Building the Foundation

The foundations of online engagement are not built overnight. They require patience, persistence, and an unwavering commitment to your audience. By understanding who they are, tapping into the psychology of interaction, crafting an authentic voice, and choosing the right platforms, you create the groundwork for relationships that go beyond transactions.

Engagement is not just a metric; it is the heartbeat of your brand's success. As you build upon these foundations, you'll find that the rewards—loyalty, advocacy, and growth—are well worth the effort.

1.1 Defining Your Audience: Who Are They and What Do They Want?

Knowing the Soul of Your Audience

Every thriving brand begins with a deep understanding of its audience. Imagine your business as a ship navigating uncharted waters. Without knowing who your audience is, your efforts are like sailing blind, vulnerable to being swept off course by every whim of the tide. But when you understand your audience—their dreams, fears, values, and desires—you hold the compass that points to success.

Defining your audience goes beyond creating generic customer personas or targeting demographics like age and location. It's about grasping the nuances that make people tick. Who are they at their core? What keeps them up at night? What sparks their joy? The answers to these questions are not static; they evolve, shaped by cultural trends, personal growth, and world events. Your task is to remain attuned to these shifts, ensuring your brand stays relevant and empathetic.

The Journey to Understanding

Understanding your audience begins with observation and research, but it grows through empathy and engagement. The data you collect—analytics from your website, interactions on social media, or responses from surveys—paints an initial portrait. However, data alone is not enough. To truly connect, you need to humanize the numbers.

Spend time engaging directly with your audience. Read their comments, respond to their questions, and listen to their stories. If you run a fitness brand, listen to how your followers talk about their health journeys. If you operate in tech, notice how your audience discusses the challenges they face with emerging tools. Their words are your guide.

As you listen, patterns will emerge. You'll notice recurring themes—shared goals, frustrations, and aspirations. These are the threads that connect your audience and offer insight into what they truly want. It's in these details that the magic of engagement lies.

Beyond Wants: Understanding Needs

While wants are the desires people express—"I want a faster phone," "I want more time"—needs are the underlying motivations driving those desires. People don't just want a faster phone; they want the efficiency it brings to their lives. They don't just want more time; they want the freedom to focus on what matters most.

When you understand the needs beneath the wants, you can position your brand not just as a product or service, but as a solution. This approach builds trust and loyalty, as your audience sees you not only selling but solving.

The Art of Listening and Adapting

Defining your audience is not a one-time task. It's a dynamic process requiring constant listening and adaptation. As trends shift and new generations emerge, your audience's values and expectations may transform. By staying curious and flexible, you ensure your brand remains in tune with its evolving identity.

One of the most overlooked tools in this process is feedback. Never underestimate the power of asking your audience what they want. Whether through polls, reviews, or informal conversations, their insights can illuminate opportunities you hadn't considered. A brand that listens is a brand that thrives.

Building a Lasting Connection

Defining your audience is not just about selling—it's about connecting. When you truly understand your audience, you can craft messages that resonate, create products that fulfill genuine needs, and foster relationships that go beyond transactions.

Your audience is the lifeblood of your business. To know them deeply is to honor them. When you embrace the art of understanding, you don't just sell to your audience; you serve them. And in that service lies the foundation for enduring success.

1.2 The Psychology of Online Interaction

The Digital Stage: Why We Connect Online

The internet has evolved into a vast, sprawling network where billions of people interact daily. Yet, despite its infinite scale, the psychology driving online interaction is surprisingly personal and deeply human. At its core, online interaction mirrors the desires and motivations that govern face-to-face communication: the need for connection, validation, and understanding.

People engage online because it offers a stage—a place to express themselves, share their stories, and feel seen. Unlike traditional forms of communication, the digital world adds layers of immediacy and accessibility. A tweet, a comment, or alike can create a sense of belonging in seconds, even between strangers continents apart. But what makes these interactions meaningful? The answer lies in understanding the psychological triggers that drive behavior in the online space.

Curiosity: The Gateway to Engagement

Humans are inherently curious beings. The lure of the unknown, the promise of discovering something new, is a powerful motivator. Online platforms thrive because they continuously feed this curiosity. Scrolling through a feed, watching a recommended video, or diving into a trending topic are all fueled by the brain's desire to explore and uncover.

For brands, tapping into this psychological driver means creating content that sparks intrigue. A question posed in a post, a mystery hinted at in a video, or a story with a compelling hook invites the audience to engage further. The key is to balance curiosity with clarity—intrigue should lead to satisfaction, not frustration. When done well, curiosity can transform passive viewers into active participants.

Validation: The Power of Recognition

Validation is one of the most potent forces in online interaction. People are drawn to spaces where they feel acknowledged and appreciated. A simple "like" on a comment or a personalized response to a question can create a lasting impression. In these moments, people don't just feel heard—they feel valued.

This principle is particularly important for brands aiming to build loyal communities. Responding to a follower's post, sharing user-generated content, or highlighting customer success stories are not just gestures—they are strategies rooted in psychology. Validation fosters trust, and trust is the bedrock of meaningful engagement.

Belonging: The Heart of Community

At its essence, the internet is a network of communities. From niche forums to global social media platforms, people seek spaces where they can connect with others who share their interests, values, and experiences. This need for belonging is deeply ingrained in human nature and is amplified in the digital world, where barriers of distance and accessibility are dissolved.

Successful brands recognize this and position themselves as facilitators of connection. They don't just sell products; they create spaces where their audience feels a sense of belonging. Whether through exclusive groups, interactive events, or relatable content, fostering community builds deeper, more emotional connections with your audience.

The Dopamine Effect: Why Engagement is Addictive

Engagement in the online world is driven by an invisible reward system rooted in brain chemistry. Each notification, comment, or share triggers a release of dopamine—a neurotransmitter associated with pleasure and reward. This creates a cycle of interaction, as people are drawn back to their devices for the next hit of validation or connection.

For brands, understanding the dopamine effect means being intentional about the timing and nature of interactions. Regular, meaningful engagement—not spammy or shallow—keeps your audience coming back, not because they feel manipulated, but because they feel genuinely connected.

Harnessing Psychology for Authentic Interaction

The psychology of online interaction is not about tricking or manipulating your audience—it's about meeting them where they are and understanding what drives them. By aligning your strategies with the principles of curiosity, validation, belonging, and reward, you can create an online presence that resonates deeply.

In this digital age, engagement is more than a marketing goal; it is a human connection forged through screens. When you understand the psychology behind these interactions, you can craft experiences that are not only impactful but unforgettable.

1.3 Crafting Your Brand's Voice: Authenticity and Relatability

The Soul of Your Brand

In the crowded digital marketplace, your brand's voice is more than just the words you use—it is the personality of your business. It reflects your values, your mission, and how you make people feel. A well-crafted voice can be the difference between a forgettable brand and one that resonates deeply with its audience. It is the soul of your brand, and when done right, it has the power to inspire trust, loyalty, and lasting connections.

But what makes a brand's voice truly impactful? The answer lies in two critical elements: authenticity and relatability. These are not mere buzzwords; they are the foundation of modern communication. In an age where audiences are savvier and more skeptical than ever, a voice that feels genuine and approachable is the key to engagement.

The Power of Authenticity

Authenticity is the currency of trust. It is what separates brands that feel human from those that come across as cold or calculated. Being authentic doesn't mean revealing every detail of your business or adopting an overly casual tone—it means being true to your values and consistent in your messaging.

Consider how you respond to a friend who speaks with honesty versus someone who seems to have ulterior motives. The same principle applies to brands. Audiences can sense when a message is forced or inauthentic, and they are quick to disengage. On the other hand, a brand that admits mistakes shares its journey, and celebrates its successes with humility is one that audiences are drawn to.

The beauty of authenticity is that it allows you to connect with your audience on a deeper level. People want to see the human side of your business—the challenges, the victories, and the passion that drives you. When you let your authenticity shine through, your brand becomes more than a business; it becomes a story worth following.

Relatability: Speaking Their Language

While authenticity builds trust, relatability fosters connection. A relatable brand understands its audience and speaks to them in a way that feels natural. This is not about mimicking slang or forcing humor; it's about aligning your message with the values, struggles, and aspirations of the people you serve.

Think of your audience as a close friend. How would you talk to them? What kind of tone would you use? Would you lecture them, or would you invite them into a conversation? Relatability is about empathy—putting yourself in their shoes and crafting a voice that feels familiar and welcoming.

When Nike tells its audience to "Just Do It," it's not just selling shoes; it's speaking to the universal desire to overcome challenges. When Dove celebrates "Real Beauty," it's not just marketing soap; it's resonating with people's need for self-acceptance. These brands understand their audiences and use their voices to create a sense of shared identity.

Finding Your Unique Voice

Crafting a brand's voice is not a one-size-fits-all process. It requires introspection and a clear understanding of your brand's identity. What do you stand for? What emotions do you want to evoke? Your voice should be a reflection of your values, your audience, and the unique space you occupy in the market.

Consistency is key. Whether it's a tweet, a blog post, or a customer service email, your voice should feel cohesive and recognizable. At the same time, allows for flexibility. A campaign about a serious issue might require a more somber tone, while a playful product launch can showcase your brand's fun side.

Building a Legacy Through Voice

A compelling brand voice does more than drive engagement—it builds a legacy. It creates a narrative that people want to be part of, a story they are eager to share. When your voice is authentic and relatable, it doesn't just attract customers; it creates advocates. These are the people who champion your brand, not because you asked them to, but because they believe in what you stand for.

Your voice is your bridge to your audience. Speak authentically, speak with empathy, and watch as your words transform transactions into relationships and relationships into loyalty. In the end, it's not just about being heard; it's about being remembered.

1.4 Tools and Platforms: Choosing the Right Channels

The Digital Landscape: Where Conversations Begin

In the vast world of online marketing, tools, and platforms are the conduits through which brands communicate with their audience. They are the digital stages where stories unfold, relationships form, and communities thrive. But not all platforms are created equal, and the tools you choose can significantly impact your ability to connect effectively.

Choosing the right channels isn't about chasing trends or being everywhere at once. It's about intentionality. It's about understanding where your audience spends their time, how they interact, and which tools best amplify your message. A thoughtful approach ensures your resources are used efficiently, and your efforts resonate with the right people.

Knowing Your Audience's Habits

Every great strategy begins with understanding your audience. The platforms they use and the tools they prefer reveal a lot about their habits and preferences. A younger demographic might gravitate toward TikTok for short-form, visually engaging content, while professionals might lean on LinkedIn for industry insights and networking.

Dive deep into audience analytics to uncover these habits. What platforms generate the most traffic to your website? Where do you receive the highest engagement? By identifying these hotspots, you can focus your energy on the channels that matter most. The goal is not just to reach your audience but to meet them in the spaces they already inhabit.

The Importance of Platform Alignment

Each platform has its unique strengths, and your choice should align with your brand's goals and the type of content you create. Instagram, for instance, is a visual playground, perfect for stunning imagery, behind-the-scenes glimpses, and storytelling through reels. Facebook excels at fostering community through groups and long-form content. Twitter, on the other hand, is a hub for real-time updates, quick insights, and direct engagement.

Your brand's voice must adapt to the nuances of each platform while remaining consistent in its core identity. A playful, vibrant tone might thrive on Instagram but require a more polished delivery on LinkedIn. By tailoring your approach, you maximize the impact of your message while maintaining brand integrity.

Essential Tools for Amplification

Beyond the platforms, tools play a critical role in streamlining your efforts and enhancing engagement. Social media scheduling tools like Hootsuite or Buffer allow you to plan content efficiently, while analytics platforms like Google Analytics or Sprout Social provide valuable insights into performance and audience behavior.

For content creation, tools like Canva simplify design for non-creatives, and platforms like Adobe Creative Suite empower you to craft professional-grade visuals. Video editing tools such as CapCut or Final Cut Pro can elevate your storytelling, while email marketing platforms like Mailchimp help you nurture leads and build long-term connections.

The key is to use tools that complement your strategy, not overwhelm it. Technology should serve as an enabler, not a distraction. Choose tools that fit seamlessly into your workflow and focus on those that provide the highest return on investment.

Quality Over Quantity

One of the biggest mistakes brands make is spreading themselves too thin. Trying to maintain a presence on every platform often dilutes the quality of content and drains resources. Instead, prioritize depth over breadth. It's better to excel on two or three platforms than to deliver mediocre results across ten.

This focus ensures you can create tailored, high-quality content that resonates with your audience. Engagement is not just about showing up—it's about showing up with purpose. When you focus your energy on the right channels, your impact grows exponentially.

Adapting to Change

The digital world evolves rapidly, with new platforms and tools emerging regularly. What works today may not work tomorrow, which is why adaptability is crucial. Stay informed about trends and be willing to experiment, but always return to your core question: does this serve my audience and align with my goals?

When Threads debuted as a text-based social platform, brands that had a clear strategy adapted quickly, leveraging the platform to enhance conversations. Others hesitated, unsure of its fit. Success lies in balancing exploration with a firm understanding of your identity.

Building Your Digital Ecosystem

Your choice of tools and platforms is the foundation of your online presence. Together, they create a digital ecosystem that supports your brand's growth. By understanding your audience, aligning your platforms with your goals, and leveraging the right tools, you can craft a strategy that amplifies your voice and strengthens your connection with your community.

The digital stage is vast, but with the right channels, your brand doesn't just find its place—it shines.

Chapter 2: Building and Nurturing Online Communities

The Heartbeat of Connection

An online community is more than a collection of followers; it is the lifeblood of your brand's digital presence. It's where trust is cultivated, ideas are exchanged, and relationships are forged. Building an online community is not just a strategy—it's a commitment to creating a space where your audience feels valued, heard, and inspired.

In today's hyperconnected world, people crave authenticity and a sense of belonging. They gravitate toward communities that resonate with their values, where their voices matter. As a brand, your role is to be the facilitator of these connections, the anchor that draws like-minded individuals together. This requires more than merely broadcasting your message. It demands active participation, genuine care, and a vision that unites your audience with a common purpose.

Laying the Foundation

The first step in building a community is defining its purpose. Ask yourself, why would someone join? What value are you offering? A community without a clear mission is like a ship without a rudder, drifting aimlessly. Whether you aim to educate, inspire, entertain, or support, your purpose should guide every interaction and decision.

Once you've defined your purpose, choose the right platform to host your community. Facebook Groups, Discord servers, and LinkedIn communities each offer unique features suited to different audiences. If your brand thrives on visuals, platforms like Instagram or Pinterest might be ideal for fostering engagement. Whatever platform you choose, ensure it aligns with your audience's preferences and habits.

Consistency is the next critical step. Regular posting, timely responses, and active engagement show your audience that you're invested in the community. Consistency doesn't just build visibility; it builds trust. Over time, your presence becomes a reliable touchstone, encouraging members to participate more actively.

The Art of Engagement

A thriving community is interactive. This means moving beyond one-way communication to foster genuine dialogue. Ask questions, solicit feedback, and encourage members to share their stories. People are more likely to engage when they feel their contributions matter.

Storytelling is a powerful tool in this regard. Share anecdotes, case studies, or behind-the-scenes glimpses that humanize your brand. When members see the people behind the product, they're more likely to relate to and trust your mission.

Recognize and celebrate your community members. Highlight user-generated content, share member successes, or simply acknowledge active participants. This creates a sense of appreciation, making members feel like integral parts of the group.

Nurturing Long-Term Growth

Building a community is not a one-time effort; it's an ongoing journey. As your community grows, so do its needs. Listen closely to your members. Their feedback can offer valuable insights into how to evolve your content, services, or approach.

Set goals to measure progress. Growth can be measured not only in numbers but in the quality of engagement. Are members participating more actively? Are they sharing your content? These indicators reflect the health of your community and help you identify areas for improvement.

Adaptability is key. Trends change, platforms evolve, and audience expectations shift. Stay flexible, experimenting with new ideas and formats while staying true to your core purpose. Growth is not just about expanding your audience but deepening the connections you've already built.

The Ripple Effect of Community

A well-nurtured online community does more than serve its members; it amplifies your brand's reach and impact. Loyal members become advocates, sharing their message with others and bringing in new voices. They offer testimonials, spread word-of-mouth, and create organic growth that no marketing campaign can replicate.

More importantly, a vibrant community enriches its members' lives. It provides a space for learning, support, and collaboration, fostering relationships that extend beyond the screen. This emotional connection is what transforms a brand into a movement.

Building and nurturing an online community is not easy, but it is profoundly rewarding. When done with care and intention, it becomes the heart of your brand, a testament to the power of genuine connection in the digital age.

2.1 What Makes a Community Thrive? Core Principles of Connection

The Pulse of a Thriving Community

A thriving community is alive with energy and purpose. It is not simply a collection of individuals but a dynamic network of relationships, a shared space where people come together to exchange ideas, offer support, and celebrate common interests. At its heart, a thriving community is one that feels alive because it is built on meaningful connections. But what is it that makes some communities flourish while others fizzle out?

The answer lies in understanding the core principles of connection. These principles serve as the foundation upon which successful communities are built and nurtured. By fostering trust, inclusivity, shared purpose, and active engagement, you can create an environment where members feel valued and inspired to participate.

The Power of Trust

Trust is the bedrock of any thriving community. Without it, engagement is superficial at best. Trust allows members to feel safe, both in expressing their thoughts and in relying on others. This psychological safety is crucial, as it encourages open communication and vulnerability.

To cultivate trust, transparency is key. Be clear about the community's purpose, rules, and expectations. As a leader, show consistency in your actions and decisions. When conflicts arise, address them promptly and fairly. Trust is not built overnight, but with time and effort, it becomes the glue that holds your community together.

Inclusivity: Welcoming All Voices

Inclusivity transforms a community from a group of participants into a true collective. When members feel seen and valued for who they are, they are more likely to contribute and connect with others. Inclusivity means more than avoiding exclusion; it means actively welcoming diverse voices, perspectives, and experiences.

Consider the tone of your interactions and the accessibility of your platform. Does your community feel open to new members? Are you addressing the unique needs of different groups within your audience? By fostering an environment where everyone feels they belong, you create a community that thrives on its richness of ideas and experiences.

Shared Purpose: The North Star

Every thriving community needs a guiding light, a shared purpose that brings its members together. Whether it's a mutual passion, a common goal, or a unifying mission, this purpose is what gives the community its identity and direction. Without it, members may struggle to see the value in staying engaged.

Articulate your community's purpose clearly and revisit it regularly. Encourage members to share their own stories about how the community's mission resonates with them. A well-defined purpose creates a sense of alignment, inspiring members to invest their time and energy into collective success.

Active Engagement: Participation as Oxygen

Engagement is the lifeblood of a thriving community. It's not enough to simply attract members; you must inspire them to participate. Active engagement transforms passive observers into contributors, creating a ripple effect that energizes the entire group.

Foster engagement by asking thought-provoking questions, encouraging collaboration, and celebrating member achievements. Show up consistently and lead by example. Engagement isn't about demanding participation—it's about creating opportunities for members to naturally express themselves and connect with others.

The Role of Leadership

Behind every successful community is intentional leadership. As a leader, your role is to guide, support, and empower. Leadership in a thriving community isn't about control; it's about facilitation. You set the tone, model the values, and ensure the environment remains conducive to growth and connection.

Good leaders listen more than they speak. They observe the needs of their community and adapt accordingly. They know when to step in and when to step back, allowing members to take the reins and shape the community's direction.

The Ripple Effect of Connection

When a community thrives, its impact extends beyond its borders. Members carry the energy of their interactions into their lives, becoming ambassadors for the values and mission of the group. These ripple effects can lead to organic growth, increased loyalty, and opportunities for collaboration that would have been unimaginable in isolation.

Thriving communities are not born—they are cultivated. By anchoring your efforts in trust, inclusivity, shared purpose, and engagement, you can create a space that not only attracts members but also inspires them to stay, participate, and contribute to something greater than themselves. In the end, a thriving community is not just a destination; it is a journey of collective connection and growth.

2.2 Creating Value: Content, Collaboration, and Communication

The Essence of Value

In the crowded digital landscape, value is the currency that sets your community apart. It is what draws members to your space, keeps them engaged, and inspires them to return time and time. Value isn't just about what you provide; it's about what your audience perceives as meaningful. To build a thriving community, you must master the art of creating value through content, collaboration, and communication.

At its core, creating value is about meeting your audience's needs while exceeding their expectations. It's not enough to offer content or services; you must craft experiences that resonate deeply, foster growth, and build lasting connections. When your community members feel they gain something significant—be it knowledge, inspiration, or a sense of belonging—they become loyal participants and enthusiastic advocates.

Content as the Cornerstone

Content is the foundation of value in any online community. Whether it's educational articles, engaging videos, or thought-provoking discussions, content provides the substance that fuels your community's interactions. However, not all content is created equal. To truly create value, your content must be relevant, high-quality, and aligned with your audience's interests.

Start by understanding your audience's needs and aspirations. Are they seeking practical advice, inspiration, or entertainment? Tailor your content to address these desires, ensuring every piece serves a purpose. Regularly update your offerings to stay fresh and relevant, keeping your community engaged and excited.

Storytelling is a powerful tool in content creation. By weaving narratives that connect emotionally with your audience, you can create content that not only informs but also inspires. Share real-life examples, success stories, or behind-the-scenes insights that humanize your brand and foster a sense of authenticity.

The Power of Collaboration

Collaboration breathes life into a community, transforming it from a one-way exchange into a dynamic network of interactions. By involving your members in content creation and decision-making, you empower them to take ownership of the community's direction.

Invite guest contributors to share their expertise or perspectives. Collaborative projects, such as co-created content or group challenges, not only generate fresh ideas but also strengthen the bonds between members. When individuals see their contributions recognized and valued, they feel a deeper connection to the community.

Partnerships can also enhance collaboration. Partnering with influencers, organizations, or industry experts can bring new voices and resources to your community, expanding its reach and appeal. Collaboration is not just about sharing the spotlight; it's about amplifying the collective value you offer.

Communication as the Lifeline

Communication is the glue that holds a community together. It's how you listen, respond, and foster dialogue. Effective communication goes beyond broadcasting messages—it involves active listening, empathy, and meaningful interaction.

Engage with your members regularly, responding to their comments, questions, and concerns. Create opportunities for open dialogue through live Q&A sessions, discussion threads, or virtual events. By showing genuine interest in your members' voices, you strengthen their trust and loyalty.

Clarity and consistency are vital in communication. Ensure your messaging aligns with your community's values and purpose. Whether you're sharing updates, providing feedback, or addressing challenges, your tone should always reflect respect and understanding.

When value is at the heart of your community, its impact extends far beyond individual members. Valuable content sparks conversations, collaborative efforts inspire innovation, and meaningful communication fosters a sense of belonging. Together, these elements create a virtuous cycle of growth, loyalty, and engagement.

By focusing on content, collaboration, and communication, you lay the groundwork for a community that thrives on shared value. This is not just about meeting needs—it's about enriching lives. When your community feels genuinely valued, it becomes a vibrant, enduring space where members want to invest their time, energy, and passion.

2.3 Strategies for Active Participation and Engagement

Beyond Passive Membership

Building an online community is a remarkable achievement, but the true magic lies in fostering active participation. A thriving community is one where members don't just observe from the sidelines; they engage, share, and contribute. Encouraging active participation isn't about coercion or flashy gimmicks—it's about creating an environment where people feel inspired to connect and compelled to interact.

Active participation breathes life into a community, transforming it from a static space into a dynamic ecosystem. It enhances the value of every interaction, strengthens member bonds, and fosters a sense of belonging that no marketing strategy alone can replicate. To achieve this, you need strategies rooted in authenticity, creativity, and understanding of human behavior.

Cultivating a Sense of Ownership

When members feel like they are co-creators of a community, their participation becomes natural and enthusiastic. This sense of ownership is cultivated by empowering members to play an active role in shaping the group's direction.

Invite your audience to contribute ideas, vote on decisions, or take part in collaborative projects. For example, let members suggest topics for discussion or submit questions for Q&A sessions. Recognize and highlight these contributions, showcasing that their voices matter. A community built with its members, rather than for them, fosters pride and engagement.

Creating roles or responsibilities within the group also encourages deeper involvement. Designate moderators, event organizers, or ambassadors who help maintain the community and drive its activities. These roles not only foster participation but also enhance the community's structure and sustainability.

Encouraging Conversations That Matter

Conversations are the heart of any engaged community. To encourage dialogue, you need to create opportunities for meaningful discussions. Surface-level interactions may entertain, but they rarely inspire long-term commitment.

Pose open-ended questions that invite thoughtful responses. Instead of asking, "What's your favorite feature of our product?" ask, "How has this product impacted your daily life?" By prompting members to share stories, you unlock a deeper layer of connection and engagement.

Timing also plays a key role in sparking conversations. Align topics with relevant trends, events, or moments in your audience's lives. This ensures discussions feel timely and engaging, encouraging members to jump in.

Gamifying Engagement

Incorporating elements of gamification is an excellent way to encourage participation without feeling forced. People naturally enjoy rewards and recognition, so creating challenges, competitions, or incentives can make engagement fun and rewarding.

Introduce leaderboards, badges, or points for active members who contribute frequently. Offer exclusive perks for participation, such as access to special content, giveaways, or insider events. Gamification should always feel like an enhancement, not a distraction from the community's primary purpose.

Leading by Example

As a community leader, your participation sets the tone. Active engagement on your part shows members that the community is a priority and worth their time. Regularly interact with posts, respond to comments, and share updates to demonstrate your investment.

Your leadership also shapes the culture of the group. If you model curiosity, positivity, and genuine care, members will follow suit. By showing vulnerability and sharing your own experiences, you invite others to do the same, creating a culture of openness and trust.

Building Consistent Engagement

Consistency is the cornerstone of sustained participation. Sporadic efforts lead to disengagement, so establish a rhythm that members can rely on. Schedule regular events, like live chats, webinars, or themed discussions. Consistent touchpoints keep your community active and ensure members have something to look forward to.

Variety also keeps engagement fresh. Mix up formats and activities to appeal to different preferences within your audience. Alternate between visual content, interactive polls, deep-dive discussions, and casual chats. This diversity keeps participation dynamic and inclusive.

Turning Engagement into Loyalty

Active participation is the pathway to loyalty. When members feel seen, heard, and valued, they don't just engage—they invest. They become ambassadors, advocates, and contributors who carry your community's spirit beyond its boundaries.

By fostering ownership, meaningful dialogue, and consistent interaction, you create an ecosystem where participation isn't just encouraged; it's instinctive. Your community becomes a space members don't just visit—they live in, returning again and again for the connections, value, and shared purpose they can't find elsewhere.

2.4 Handling Challenges: Conflict Resolution and Moderation

Navigating the Storm

In any thriving community, conflicts are inevitable. Disagreements, misunderstandings, and clashes of opinion can arise, especially when diverse voices come together. Rather than viewing these moments as setbacks, the key lies in how you handle them. Conflict, when managed effectively, can strengthen a community by fostering mutual understanding, trust, and growth. As a leader, learning the art of conflict resolution and moderation is essential to maintain the integrity and harmony of your community.

The goal is not to avoid conflict but to create an environment where it can be addressed constructively. Whether it's a heated argument in the comments, a difference in opinion during a discussion, or an issue with a member's behavior, your approach to resolution sets the tone for the community.

Setting Clear Expectations

The foundation of effective conflict resolution lies in clarity. Before issues arise, establish clear guidelines that define acceptable behavior and the values your community upholds. These rules should be easily accessible to all members, with a clear understanding that respect, empathy, and constructive dialogue are paramount.

Setting expectations allows members to understand the boundaries within which they are expected to operate. When conflict does arise, it's easier to address it if everyone knows the community's code of conduct and has been reminded of it regularly. By preemptively creating a culture of respect, you set the stage for smoother resolutions.

The Power of Active Listening

When conflict emerges, the first step toward resolution is to listen. Often, the root of a problem lies in a lack of understanding, and by listening attentively, you create an environment where members feel heard and valued. Listening is not just about hearing words; it's about understanding feelings, motivations, and underlying concerns.

Encourage those involved in the conflict to express their perspectives fully, without interruption or judgment. By allowing space for these conversations, you not only resolve the issue at hand but also build trust within the community. Members will appreciate a leader who listens empathetically, creating a sense of security and fairness.

Mediating and Finding Common Ground

Once you have listened to all parties involved, it's time to step in as a mediator. Your role is not to take sides but to find common ground. Encourage both parties to focus on shared goals or mutual interests.

Frame the conversation in a way that highlights the community's values and the importance of working together. Remind the members involved that while disagreements are natural, they should always be approached with respect for one another. Through thoughtful questioning and reframing, you can guide both sides toward a resolution that is constructive and amicable.

In some cases, it may be necessary to take a more direct approach. If a member is continuously disruptive or violating community guidelines, a private conversation may be required. In these situations, maintain professionalism and kindness, focusing on how their actions affect the community and offering clear steps for improvement.

Moderation: The Silent Force

While conflict resolution is often about personal intervention, moderation is the silent force that maintains community order. Moderation ensures that conversations stay on track, preventing negativity from spiraling out of control and keeping the environment safe for all members.

As a leader, moderation goes beyond enforcing rules; it's about setting the tone for how members interact with one another. Lead by example, offering constructive feedback, guiding discussions, and stepping in when necessary to prevent harmful behavior.

It's also important to equip trusted members with moderation tools. Empower your team of moderators to step in when they spot potential issues, offering guidance and support. A well-moderated community runs smoothly, where everyone feels safe to express their thoughts without fear of harassment or negativity.

Turning Challenges into Growth Opportunities

Conflict, while often uncomfortable, can lead to significant growth if approached the right way. By addressing issues openly and fairly, you not only resolve the immediate problem but also set the stage for a more resilient and united community.

Each conflict handled with care strengthens the foundation of trust. Members come to appreciate a community that is willing to navigate challenges with respect and understanding. Ultimately, a well-moderated space, where issues are addressed thoughtfully and inclusively, fosters a deeper sense of connection and belonging.

By embracing conflict resolution and moderation as tools for growth, you ensure your community remains a space where open dialogue, respect, and collaboration thrive. Through thoughtful management, even the most challenging moments can transform into opportunities for deeper engagement and stronger connections.

Chapter 3: The Rise of Micro-Influencers

The Power of the Small but Mighty

In the world of online marketing, the landscape has shifted dramatically. Gone are the days when celebrity endorsements were the only path to widespread influence. Today, a new force has emerged that is reshaping the way businesses connect with audiences: the micro-influencer. While their following may not rival that of global superstars, their impact is proving to be even more profound.

Micro-influencers are individuals with a smaller, yet highly engaged, following—typically between 1,000 and 100,000 followers on social media platforms. Their authenticity, relatability, and deep connections with their audience make them powerful tools in the arsenal of modern marketing. The rise of the micro-influencer represents a profound shift in how businesses approach influence and brand advocacy.

Authenticity in a Sea of Noise

The reason behind the explosive growth of micro-influencers lies in their ability to foster authentic connections with their followers. In an age where consumers are bombarded by constant advertisements and sponsored content, people are becoming more discerning. They crave genuine, trustworthy recommendations from sources they feel they know personally.

Micro-influencers thrive in this environment because they maintain a sense of authenticity. They're often seen as real people who share unfiltered glimpses of their lives, whether it's their daily routines, passions, or struggles. This rawness and vulnerability create a bond of trust that larger influencers, who may appear more polished and distant, struggle to replicate. For businesses, this means that their products or services are not just being promoted—they are being endorsed by individuals who come across as relatable and trustworthy.

Engaging Niche Audiences

Another compelling aspect of micro-influencers is their ability to target niche audiences with laser precision. Unlike celebrities who cast a wide net, micro-influencers typically cater to specific interests or communities, whether it's fitness enthusiasts, book lovers, gamers, or eco-conscious consumers.

This focus on niche markets allows brands to tailor their marketing strategies to specific groups, creating a more personalized and relevant message. When a micro-influencer promotes a product to its audience, it resonates deeply because that product aligns with the interests, values, or lifestyles of the followers. For businesses, this means reaching the right people with the right message, significantly increasing the chances of conversion.

The Cost-Effectiveness of Micro-Influencers

For many businesses, especially small and medium-sized enterprises, budget constraints make it difficult to compete with larger brands that can afford to hire high-profile influencers. Micro-influencers, however, offer a more cost-effective solution. Their fees are often significantly lower than those of big-name celebrities, yet their impact can be just as powerful.

Studies have shown that micro-influencers often deliver higher engagement rates than their more famous counterparts. Their followers are not only more likely to see their content, but they are also more likely to interact with it. This means that even with a smaller following, a micro-influencer can generate a greater return on investment for businesses looking to expand their reach without breaking the bank.

The Trust Factor: Building Long-Term Relationships

The success of micro-influencer marketing is largely built on trust. When a micro-influencer recommends a product, their followers perceive the endorsement as genuine, rather than a paid promotion. This trust translates into loyalty, which is a powerful asset for brands.

For businesses, working with micro-influencers is not just a one-time transaction—it's the beginning of a long-term relationship. Unlike traditional advertising or influencer partnerships that may be short-lived, micro-influencers often form lasting bonds with the brands they endorse. These partnerships are built on mutual respect and shared values, creating a natural alignment between the brand and its audience.

Harnessing the Power of Micro-Influencers

As businesses continue to adapt to the evolving digital landscape, understanding the role of micro-influencers is essential. They offer a unique combination of authenticity, niche targeting, cost-effectiveness, and trust that larger influencers simply cannot replicate.

For brands seeking to engage with their audience in a meaningful way, micro-influencers are a powerful tool. By embracing these small but mighty voices, businesses can connect with consumers on a deeper level, create long-lasting relationships, and ultimately drive growth. In a world where authenticity is currency, the rise of micro-influencers marks a new era of marketing—one that values genuine connections over superficial endorsements.

3.1 Who Are Micro-Influencers and Why They Matter

The New Face of Influence

In a world where social media feeds are flooded with content from celebrities, influencers, and brands, a new class of digital trendsetters has emerged: micro-influencers. While they may not have millions of followers like their A-list counterparts, micro-influencers are shaping the future of marketing in ways that are far more intimate, impactful, and sustainable. With followings ranging from 1,000 to 100,000, they may seem small in comparison to the social media megastars, but their ability to engage and influence is anything but.

Micro-influencers are everyday people who have built a reputation within a specific niche. Whether it's fitness, fashion, travel, food, or technology, these individuals have a highly engaged audience who views them not as distant figures, but as relatable, trustworthy sources of information. Unlike traditional celebrities, micro-influencers maintain an air of authenticity that resonates deeply with their followers.

The Authentic Connection

What sets micro-influencers apart is their ability to cultivate real, authentic relationships with their followers. Unlike polished, scripted posts from larger influencers, micro-influencers often share unfiltered, genuine content that offers a window into their daily lives. Their posts tend to be more personal and less commercialized, making it easier for followers to connect with them on a human level.

In a digital age saturated with advertising, consumers are increasingly skeptical of traditional marketing tactics. People no longer want to be sold to—they want to be engaged, informed, and entertained. This is where micro-influencers shine. Their followers trust them not only for their expertise but also for their relatability. When a micro-influencer shares a product or service, it doesn't feel like an ad. It feels like a recommendation from a friend.

Why Micro-Influencers Matter to Brands

For businesses, micro-influencers present a goldmine of opportunities. Their ability to build tight-knit communities of loyal followers means that brands can tap into a highly targeted audience that is primed for conversion. While larger influencers boast vast reach, micro-influencers excel in deep engagement. They're able to communicate directly with their audience, sparking conversations and driving interactions that larger influencers often struggle to maintain.

The beauty of working with micro-influencers is their ability to speak directly to niche markets. Whether it's vegan skincare, home decor, or niche hobbies, micro-influencers help brands tailor their messaging to a specific group of consumers. For businesses, this means better-targeted marketing efforts that speak to the people who matter most—those with the interests and purchasing power that align with the brand's offerings.

The Cost-Effectiveness Factor

Another reason micro-influencers matter is their cost-effectiveness. While larger influencers command sky-high fees for brand collaborations, micro-influencers are much more affordable, often charging a fraction of the price. This accessibility opens up opportunities for small and mid-sized businesses to enter the influencer marketing space without breaking the bank.

Despite their smaller following, micro-influencers often deliver better engagement rates and higher return on investment (ROI). Their followers are more likely to comment, like, and share their posts, creating an organic ripple effect that spreads brand awareness. Research has shown that micro-influencers often generate more conversations around products and services than their more famous counterparts, leading to greater brand visibility and consumer loyalty.

The Power of Trust

At the core of micro-influencer marketing is trust. When a micro-influencer endorses a product, their audience believes it because they trust the influencer's opinion. This trust is invaluable in the world of online marketing. People are more likely to act on recommendations from those they feel are authentic, making micro-influencers a powerful force in influencing purchasing decisions.

Unlike traditional advertising, which often feels one-sided, micro-influencers foster two-way communication. They engage with their followers regularly, responding to comments, asking for feedback, and creating a sense of community. This back-and-forth exchange builds a deeper level of trust, leading to increased loyalty and higher conversion rates.

Shaping the Future of Marketing

In the ever-evolving world of social media, micro-influencers are shaping the future of marketing. Their authenticity, relatability, and deep connections with their audience make them an indispensable asset to any brand looking to create meaningful relationships with consumers. As consumers continue to demand more personalized and genuine interactions, the rise of micro-influencers will only continue to grow, transforming the marketing landscape for years to come.

In a world where bigger is often seen as better, micro-influencers prove that sometimes the smallest voices can have the loudest impact.

3.2 Finding the Right Influencers for Your Brand

Understanding Your Brand's Values

The journey to finding the right micro-influencer begins long before you even begin to scroll through social media profiles. It begins with a deep understanding of your own brand's values, vision, and target audience. Without this clarity, your search for an influencer is like trying to find a needle in a haystack. The key is to align your brand's essence with the right person—someone whose voice and audience resonate with your own goals.

Start by identifying what makes your brand unique. Is your brand eco-conscious, promoting sustainable products? Is it trendy and cutting-edge, constantly on the pulse of new styles? Understanding what sets your brand apart will allow you to find influencers who speak to the same values. The influencers you work with should be the ones whose ethos complements yours, ensuring an authentic and seamless partnership. When your brand's message aligns with their voice, the collaboration feels natural, and the audience will feel the sincerity.

The Importance of Audience Demographics

Once you have a clear understanding of your brand's identity, the next step is to pinpoint the right audience. Micro-influencers are incredibly effective because they cater to niche groups. But not all niche groups are the same, and not all audiences are right for your brand. You need to find influencers who have a following that reflects the demographics of your ideal customers.

Begin by examining the influencer's audience. Who are they? Are they within the age group, geographic location, and income bracket that aligns with your target market? An influencer who speaks to a fitness-focused audience might not be a perfect fit for a brand that specializes in gourmet kitchen gadgets. Understanding these nuances is vital for ensuring your influencer campaign reaches the people who are most likely to purchase from your brand.

Engagement Is More Important Than Numbers

In the world of influencer marketing, there's a temptation to focus solely on follower counts. After all, the more followers an influencer has, the more potential reach there is, right? Not necessarily. The true power of an influencer lies not in their number of followers but in their engagement rate—the frequency and quality of interactions between the influencer and their audience.

A micro-influencer with 10,000 highly engaged followers can drive much higher engagement than an influencer with 100,000 followers who receive only surface-level interactions. Engagement is the true indicator of trust and loyalty. If an influencer's audience is regularly commenting, sharing, and interacting with their content, it's a clear sign that they've fostered a loyal and active community. This loyalty translates into real impact when they promote your brand.

Authenticity and Credibility Matter

An influencer's authenticity is their greatest asset, and it's essential to find influencers who maintain credibility in their niche. Authenticity isn't just about their posts being unfiltered or relatable—it's also about how genuine their endorsements are. Are they truly passionate about the products they promote, or are they just adding another paid post to their feed?

Before reaching out, review the influencer's past collaborations. Do they align with your brand? Have their sponsored posts felt natural, or do they come across as forced? An influencer who regularly promotes products unrelated to their niche risks losing credibility. Your brand deserves an influencer who aligns with your values and genuinely supports your product. This authenticity strengthens the campaign's impact and ensures that your product is showcased organically.

Building a Relationship: Moving Beyond Transactions

Finally, remember that influencer partnerships should be more than a simple transaction. Micro-influencers thrive on relationships, both with their followers and with the brands they endorse. When selecting an influencer, consider their approach to partnerships. Are they open to long-term collaborations or focused only on one-off deals?

Building a lasting relationship with an influencer allows your brand to grow alongside them. A sustained partnership deepens trust with their audience, resulting in increased brand loyalty. Instead of a fleeting campaign, this becomes an ongoing conversation, where the influencer's endorsement doesn't feel like an isolated promotion but rather an integral part of their regular content.

Finding the right influencers for your brand is not about chasing the biggest numbers or the flashiest profiles. It's about identifying individuals who embody your brand's values, connect with your target audience, and foster authentic, lasting relationships. With the right partners, micro-influencers have the power to elevate your brand in ways that feel personal, relatable, and most importantly, genuine.

3.3 Building Relationships: How to Collaborate Authentically

The Foundation of Authentic Collaboration

When it comes to influencer marketing, the most successful partnerships are those built on trust and genuine connection. The notion of "collaboration" may often be seen through a transactional lens: a brand sends products to an influencer, who then shares a post in exchange for payment. However, the real magic lies in cultivating relationships that go beyond simple transactions and foster long-term, authentic partnerships.

An authentic collaboration starts with the recognition that both the brand and the influencer bring value to the table. It's about understanding the influencer's role as not just a promoter of products but as a storyteller and community builder. As such, the relationship should be viewed as a mutual partnership rather than a one-sided exchange. By focusing on shared goals, values, and interests, brands, and influencers can create content that resonates deeply with audiences and reflects the essence of both parties.

Crafting a Shared Vision

The key to authenticity in collaboration lies in a shared vision. This doesn't mean that the brand and influencer need to have identical goals, but there should be a clear alignment in values, tone, and messaging. Before entering into a collaboration, take the time to understand the influencer's content style, the type of audience they engage with, and their core beliefs. Similarly, influencers need to understand the brand's ethos, vision, and the message they want to communicate.

When both parties align their visions, the collaboration feels organic. The influencer can present your product or service in a way that feels natural to their followers, blending seamlessly into the narrative they've already created. For example, if a travel influencer who focuses on eco-friendly travel promotes a sustainable product, their audience will recognize the alignment and respond positively. In this way, collaboration becomes a mutually beneficial effort—one that allows both the brand and influencer to grow together while delivering authentic value to the audience.

Open Communication and Flexibility

A strong, collaborative relationship is built on open communication. This involves not just discussing goals and expectations but also maintaining an ongoing dialogue throughout the process. Clear communication helps ensure that both the brand and the influencer are on the same page, preventing misunderstandings and ensuring that the collaboration stays true to its original vision.

Flexibility is another cornerstone of authentic collaboration. No two collaborations are identical, and each partnership will require some degree of adaptation. Brands should trust the influencer's creative process and give them room to add their personal touch. Remember, the influencer knows their audience better than anyone, and their voice should shine through in the content they create.

When a brand imposes rigid guidelines or controls too much of the process, it risks stifling the influencer's creativity, and in turn, undermining the authenticity of the content. A successful partnership involves balancing brand objectives with the influencer's style, ensuring that both elements are represented in the outcome.

Trust and Long-Term Engagement

Authenticity doesn't happen overnight, and neither do lasting relationships. It's easy to view influencer partnerships as short-term campaigns, but the most successful brands understand the power of long-term engagement. A brand that consistently works with the same influencer can create a deeper connection with the influencer's audience. This ongoing relationship helps to build trust over time, and when a trusted influencer repeatedly endorses a product, their audience is more likely to respond positively.

Long-term collaboration allows influencers to integrate a brand into their lifestyle, making their endorsements feel less like promotions and more like genuine recommendations. Whether it's a series of product reviews, event coverage, or behind-the-scenes glimpses of how a brand fits into their daily life, the relationship becomes more authentic the more it is nurtured.

Mutual Benefit: A Win-Win for Both Parties

The ultimate goal of authentic collaboration is to create a win-win situation for both the brand and the influencer. For the brand, this means achieving increased visibility, loyalty, and consumer trust. For the influencer, it's about maintaining their credibility and continuing to deliver valuable content to their followers.

When both parties focus on mutual benefit rather than one-sided gain, the collaboration feels less like marketing and more like a shared experience. Influencers who genuinely believe in the product they are promoting will naturally convey this belief to their audience, and their followers will appreciate the authenticity. Likewise, brands that prioritize the influencer's creative freedom and personal touch will find that the resulting content is far more impactful than a generic advertisement.

In the end, authentic collaboration isn't just about getting your product in front of more eyes; it's about building trust, respect, and lasting relationships. By taking the time to understand each other's goals and values, both brands and influencers can create something that resonates deeply with their audiences and drives real, meaningful results.

3.4 Case Studies: Success Stories in Micro-Influencer Partnerships

The Power of Personal Connections: A Skincare Brand's Transformation

In the crowded world of skincare, where giant brands dominate the market, standing out can seem like an impossible task. However, one emerging skincare company discovered the power of micro-influencers to carve out its niche and transform its brand image. Rather than opting for traditional celebrity endorsements or partnering with influencers with millions of followers, this brand focused on cultivating relationships with micro-influencers who shared a genuine passion for skincare.

The key to their success was a carefully curated strategy that placed authenticity at its heart. The brand targeted influencers with audiences between 5,000 and 50,000 followers—individuals who had already built strong relationships with their communities, particularly in beauty and self-care niches. These influencers were known for their in-depth product reviews and detailed tutorials, which helped their followers make informed purchasing decisions.

By working with these micro-influencers, the skincare brand was able to reach a highly engaged, niche audience that trusted the influencer's opinion. Each micro-influencer received products tailored to their specific skin concerns, and in turn, they shared personalized experiences with their followers. Rather than generic, one-size-fits-all content, the influencers showcased how the products integrated into their daily skincare routines. The result was a series of authentic and relatable posts that sparked real conversations, allowing the brand to engage with a community that was highly receptive to its message.

In just a few months, this brand saw a significant uptick in sales and a noticeable increase in brand awareness. The most impressive result, however, was the lasting relationship it built with both the influencers and their audiences, transforming these early collaborations into long-term partnerships. The brand's success lay not just in the immediate ROI but in the deeper, more valuable connections it made through micro-influencer partnerships.

Tapping into Niche Markets: The Rise of Sustainable Fashion

Sustainability has become a driving force in the fashion industry, but for many smaller, eco-conscious brands, breaking through the noise of fast fashion can be daunting. One sustainable fashion label, however, leveraged the power of micro-influencers to spread its message of ethical consumerism to a community of environmentally conscious shoppers.

Instead of casting a wide net, the brand strategically partnered with micro-influencers in niche sectors, such as veganism, eco-travel, and slow fashion. These influencers may not have boasted the largest follower counts, but they had deeply engaged communities that were aligned with the brand's ethos. By selecting influencers who were passionate about sustainability, the brand tapped into a highly targeted market that was both attentive and motivated to make conscious purchasing decisions.

The influencers were not just given free products to promote. They were invited to learn about the production process, the environmental benefits of the materials used, and the ethical values behind the brand's mission. In return, they created content that authentically communicated the brand's story to their followers. Some posted detailed "unboxing" videos showcasing the thoughtfulness behind the packaging, while others provided tutorials on how to style the clothes for different occasions. The brand also offered discount codes for followers, creating an incentive for the community to engage with the brand.

This strategy paid off in spades. Through these carefully selected collaborations, the fashion label saw a 200% increase in online sales within just a few months. Beyond the monetary gain, the brand received a surge in brand loyalty, as many of the influencers' followers began advocating for the brand in their own social circles. The partnership didn't feel like marketing—it felt like a genuine movement toward a more sustainable future, and that authenticity resonated with consumers.

A Travel Brand's Journey to Success

Travel brands often face the challenge of competing in a saturated market, where everyone seems to be promoting the same destinations and experiences. One such brand, however, took a different approach by partnering with micro-influencers who had dedicated followers interested in unique travel experiences, off-the-beaten-path destinations, and local culture.

Rather than focusing on influencers with massive followings, the travel brand sought out those with highly engaged communities who valued niche travel tips, adventure stories, and personal recommendations. These influencers shared their authentic travel experiences, often highlighting lesser-known locations and activities that catered to a specific audience, such as solo travelers or families seeking eco-friendly vacations.

Through collaboration, the travel brand was able to promote unique travel packages and destination experiences that were aligned with the influencers' passions. The influencers created compelling content, from Instagram stories to blog posts, that conveyed the authentic joy and excitement of their travel experiences, all while showcasing the brand's offerings. Because the influencers were trusted sources of information within their communities, the brand saw a significant increase in bookings from followers who were eager to embark on the same adventures.

This campaign also brought forth one of the most valuable aspects of micro-influencer marketing: word-of-mouth. Followers didn't just engage with the content—they actively shared it with their friends and family, encouraging others to discover the brand and its offerings. Over time, this organic growth resulted in increased customer loyalty, and the brand became known as a go-to choice for travelers seeking unique, curated experiences.

The Lasting Impact of Micro-Influencer Success

These case studies underscore a central truth: the most successful influencer partnerships are those that prioritize authenticity, mutual benefit, and long-term engagement. Micro-influencers are not just content creators; they are trusted voices within their communities, and by partnering with them, brands can access a level of genuine connection that is often difficult to achieve through traditional advertising.

When approached thoughtfully, micro-influencer partnerships can be a game-changer, enabling brands to reach highly engaged audiences, create impactful content, and build lasting relationships that endure far beyond the initial campaign.

Chapter 4: Integrating Communities and Influencers into Marketing

The Symbiotic Relationship Between Communities and Influencers

The landscape of online marketing is no longer defined solely by traditional methods of advertising. The power of word-of-mouth, shared values, and authenticity has shifted the dynamics, giving rise to a more human-centric form of marketing. This shift has created a symbiotic relationship between online communities and influencers, where both groups play a crucial role in amplifying brand messages. Understanding how to integrate these two forces into a seamless marketing strategy is the key to success.

Online communities are built on trust and engagement, and they thrive when people feel they are part of something greater than themselves.

These groups may form around shared interests, causes, or passions, creating a fertile ground for businesses to sow the seeds of genuine relationships. Micro-influencers, on the other hand, are individuals who have cultivated deep, personal connections with these communities, making them an invaluable asset for brands. By collaborating with these influencers, businesses can tap into their loyal followings and extend their reach more authentically and effectively.

The true power lies in the integration of these two elements. Instead of seeing communities and influencers as separate entities, businesses should view them as complementary. Communities can help influencers grow their brands, while influencers can provide the community with products and services that align with their values. Together, they create an ecosystem that drives engagement, fosters trust, and ultimately, leads to greater conversions.

Developing a Unified Marketing Strategy

The first step in integrating communities and influencers into your marketing strategy is to create a unified approach that speaks to both. Too often, brands make the mistake of targeting each group separately, without considering the overlap in their audiences. A successful strategy involves identifying the common values between the brand, the influencer, and the community.

For example, if your brand is focused on sustainability, collaborating with influencers who are passionate about eco-friendly living can create an immediate connection with like-minded communities. By ensuring that the influencer's content aligns with your brand's mission, you increase the chances of genuine interaction from the community. In this scenario, the influencer becomes more than just a promoter—they become an advocate for the cause.

Once this alignment is established, it's time to create content that resonates with both the community and the influencer's audience. This content should be meaningful, value-driven, and shareable. It's not enough to push products; instead, the content should tell a story, solve a problem, or provide education. The goal is to weave the brand into the fabric of the community's conversation in a way that feels natural and authentic.

Engaging the Community Through Collaborative Content

Collaborative content is one of the most powerful tools for integrating communities and influencers into your marketing efforts. This content can take many forms: co-hosted webinars, joint social media campaigns, behind-the-scenes videos, or community-driven contests. The key is to make the community feel as though they are part of the process. When a brand actively involves its audience in content creation, it fosters a sense of ownership and loyalty.

Micro-influencers excel at creating personal, relatable content that resonates deeply with their audience. By encouraging influencers to collaborate with their communities on content creation, businesses can produce material that is not only authentic but also highly engaging. For instance, a clothing brand might ask influencers and their followers to create styling videos using their products, allowing the community to showcase their creativity while promoting the brand in a subtle yet impactful way. This type of collaboration not only enhances brand visibility but also encourages active participation from the community, strengthening the bond between the brand, the influencer, and the audience.

Measuring Success Through Community-Driven Metrics

While traditional marketing metrics such as impressions and click-through rates are important, when integrating communities and influencers into your strategy, it's essential to look beyond these numbers. Engagement rates, sentiment analysis, and community growth are more telling indicators of success.

Engagement is the heartbeat of community-driven marketing. When your community is actively participating in discussions, sharing content, and providing feedback, it's a clear sign that your brand is resonating with them. Micro-influencers can provide valuable insights into how their followers are interacting with your content, offering a deeper understanding of your audience's needs and preferences.

Sentiment analysis, which gauges the emotions behind online interactions, is also a critical metric. Are people excited about your product? Do they feel connected to your brand? Positive sentiment often leads to advocacy, and when influencers share content with an overwhelmingly positive response, it amplifies the brand's credibility.

Finally, measuring community growth gives businesses a long-term view of their success. A thriving community isn't built overnight; it's a gradual process that requires consistent effort. By tracking how the community expands over time—whether through increased followers, more active discussions, or higher engagement rates—brands can assess the long-term impact of their influencer partnerships and community-building efforts.

Long-Term Integration for Sustained Growth

The integration of communities and influencers into marketing strategies is not a one-time campaign but an ongoing relationship that requires nurturing. Building lasting partnerships with influencers and actively participating in community conversations allows brands to stay relevant and maintain a strong presence in the minds of their audiences.

By continuing to provide value, engage with the community, and collaborate with trusted influencers, brands can create a sustainable cycle of growth. This long-term integration ensures that the brand doesn't just achieve short-term success, but cultivates a loyal customer base that continues to drive its success for years to come.

In the end, integrating communities and influencers is about building authentic, meaningful relationships that transcend the transactional nature of traditional marketing. When done right, it becomes a powerful engine for lasting brand growth, fueled by trust, engagement, and a shared commitment to common values.

4.1 Seamless Strategies: Combining Community Engagement with Influencer Campaigns

The Power of Integration

In the rapidly evolving world of online marketing, the ability to merge two powerful forces—community engagement and influencer campaigns—has become an essential strategy for brands seeking sustainable growth. It's no longer enough to simply run a campaign with influencers or engage with communities in isolation. The real magic happens when these two elements are thoughtfully combined to create a cohesive and impactful marketing approach.

Communities, built on shared interests, values, and passions, are powerful hubs of interaction. When you integrate these engaged individuals with influencers who share similar values and resonate with their audience, you create an ecosystem where authentic connections can flourish. The result? A campaign that feels organic, reaches the right people and inspires genuine action.

Building a Shared Vision

The first step in creating a seamless strategy between community engagement and influencer campaigns is building a shared vision. Brands must ask themselves: what are we trying to achieve with both our community and influencer collaborations? This vision must be clearly defined, as it will act as the compass that guides all activities moving forward. Whether your goal is to increase brand awareness, promote a new product, or reinforce a specific value, aligning both the community's interests and the influencer's audience is paramount.

For instance, a brand dedicated to sustainability may find great value in partnering with influencers who are already part of eco-conscious communities. The shared commitment to environmental causes strengthens the partnership, ensuring that both the influencer and the community's followers will resonate with the message. This alignment makes the campaign feel natural and not forced—something the community and influencer can stand behind with authenticity.

Crafting Cohesive Campaign Content

Once you've established a shared vision, the next step is crafting content that bridges the community's core values with the influencer's reach. The key here is to create content that speaks directly to both groups, blending the voice of the brand with the influencer's unique style. It's important to note that the content should not simply be promotional. Instead, it should engage, educate, and entertain the audience, offering something of value.

Think of it as a conversation rather than a monologue. Community members thrive on interaction and dialogue, so creating a campaign that invites them to participate is critical. For example, an influencer may host a live Q&A where the community members are encouraged to share their thoughts on the brand, ask questions, and even share personal experiences. This approach turns the campaign into an ongoing conversation rather than a one-time interaction.

Creating Opportunities for Engagement

For any campaign to thrive, engagement must be at the core. Communities want to feel seen and heard, and influencers are the perfect bridge to facilitate this connection. Influencers who genuinely engage with their followers on social media platforms help create an environment where community members feel valued.

Integrating influencers into the fabric of community engagement allows brands to scale their interactions in a way that feels personal. Rather than merely promoting products or services, influencers can serve as active participants, sparking discussions, encouraging user-generated content, and facilitating challenges or contests that encourage further interaction.

For example, imagine a brand running a campaign that invites both influencers and community members to create content around a specific theme, using a unique hashtag. This can generate excitement and allow everyone, including followers, to participate in a meaningful way. The content created is not just for the brand, but a collaborative effort, strengthening the sense of belonging within the community while further amplifying the brand message.

Measuring Success Through Unified Metrics

While traditional marketing strategies rely heavily on metrics such as conversions and sales, combining community engagement with influencer campaigns calls for a more holistic approach to measurement. The success of a campaign should be evaluated not only through direct sales but also through community sentiment, engagement rates, and long-term brand affinity.

Monitoring how the community responds to influencer-led content, how often they engage, and the type of conversations being sparked are all invaluable insights. These metrics tell you whether your campaign is creating the kind of impact that extends beyond immediate sales goals and fosters long-term relationships with both the community and influencers.

By using both quantitative and qualitative data, brands can assess whether they are fostering a genuine connection that goes beyond the transactional. A campaign's real success lies in its ability to create lasting relationships and cultivate loyalty—a loyalty that is amplified when both the community and influencer feel invested in the brand.

The Art of Subtle Integration

Seamless integration of community engagement and influencer campaigns requires subtlety. It's about blending the marketing efforts into the organic flow of the community and the influencer's content. For the strategy to feel authentic, there must be no clear boundary between brand messaging and user interaction. The more seamlessly you can weave the two together, the more effective your campaign will be.

The magic of integrating these forces lies in creating moments of surprise and delight, where the brand feels like an organic extension of the community. When done right, the partnership between community and influencer will feel effortless, and the impact will extend far beyond the campaign itself, resulting in sustained growth, deeper relationships, and enhanced brand loyalty.

In the end, it's about creating an ecosystem where everyone benefits: the brand gains genuine, long-term advocates, the influencers get the opportunity to connect more authentically with their audience, and the community feels more deeply connected to the brand they support. The result is a seamless, sustainable marketing strategy that drives real, lasting success.

4.2 Metrics That Matter: Measuring the Impact of Your Efforts

The Challenge of Measuring Success

In the world of online marketing, especially when integrating community engagement and influencer campaigns, the question often arises: How do you measure success? While traditional marketing has clear metrics—sales figures, website traffic, and conversion rates—the digital landscape demands a more nuanced approach. Measuring the impact of your efforts requires a combination of both quantitative data and qualitative insights. These metrics not only inform you of your campaign's success but also help shape future strategies, ensuring that your brand continues to evolve and grow.

Understanding which metrics truly matter is key to evaluating the effectiveness of your efforts. A successful campaign isn't just about a short-term spike in sales or engagement, but about building long-term relationships and fostering deeper brand loyalty. So, what metrics should you focus on to get an accurate picture of your campaign's impact?

Engagement Rate: The Heartbeat of Your Community

The engagement rate is one of the most critical metrics to monitor when combining community engagement with influencer marketing. Engagement encompasses likes, shares, comments, and direct interactions—essentially, the signals that show whether your audience is actively participating with your content or just passively observing. A high engagement rate indicates that your community is not only watching but also connecting with the message and engaging with the influencers who share it.

However, engagement should be assessed more thoughtfully than simply counting likes or retweets. It's important to consider the quality of the engagement—are people having meaningful conversations in the comments? Are they sharing your content with their networks? Are they taking part in the challenges or campaigns you've launched? These are the deeper signals that reflect true interest and loyalty.

Sentiment Analysis: Understanding the Emotion Behind the Numbers

While engagement gives you a quantitative view, sentiment analysis reveals the emotional landscape of your audience. By analyzing the tone and sentiment of comments, mentions, and discussions, you gain insight into how your community feels about your brand. Are they excited, supportive, and positive, or do they express frustration and dissatisfaction? Sentiment analysis allows you to gauge the emotional connection that influencers and your community have with your brand.

This metric is especially useful for identifying potential issues early on. If there's a shift in sentiment, it's crucial to address it quickly. For example, if an influencer's campaign unintentionally triggers negative feelings among their followers, it's important to act swiftly to resolve the situation. Positive sentiment, on the other hand, is a sign that your message is resonating, creating trust and admiration.

Conversion Metrics: From Engagement to Action

Engagement and sentiment offer insights into your audience's relationship with your brand, but ultimately, conversion metrics determine whether your campaign is achieving tangible results. Conversions, whether they are purchases, sign-ups, or other actions, reflect how successful your community and influencer partnerships are in driving business outcomes.

To effectively track conversions, it's important to implement proper tracking tools, such as UTM parameters or affiliate links, to identify which parts of your campaign are driving action. Additionally, you can measure the customer journey to understand how engagement with an influencer or community content leads to conversions. Are customers coming directly from influencer posts, or are they interacting with community-driven content before taking the plunge? Understanding this flow helps you allocate resources efficiently and adjust your strategy for better results.

Return on Investment (ROI): Evaluating Campaign Value

While conversions are vital, ROI provides the clearest picture of your campaign's overall value. It's not just about how much revenue was generated, but also about the time, effort, and resources you invested in the campaign. Calculating ROI allows you to assess whether your influencer collaborations and community engagement were worth the investment and whether you should continue or scale your efforts.

ROI should be viewed not just in terms of financial outcomes but also in terms of brand equity. How much has your brand awareness grown? Has your social media following increased? Is your community more active and engaged than before? While these may not always translate directly into sales, they contribute significantly to the long-term success and sustainability of your brand.

Long-Term Impact: Building Loyalty and Advocacy

Finally, one of the most telling metrics of success is the long-term impact your campaign has on brand loyalty and advocacy. It's easy to get caught up in short-term spikes of interest or viral moments, but sustainable success is built on the foundations of brand loyalty. By tracking repeat engagement and the level of ongoing interaction from both influencers and community members, you can measure whether your campaign has cultivated a genuine, lasting connection.

Repeat customers, sustained conversation, and word-of-mouth advocacy are all indicators of a strong, loyal following. Brands that successfully integrate community and influencer marketing can expect to see this loyalty blossom, resulting in a community that actively champions the brand without any incentive other than their passion for the values you represent.

Ultimately, measuring the impact of your marketing efforts is about understanding your audience, their relationship with your brand, and how effectively your community and influencer strategies have worked together. The metrics that matter are not just numbers—they tell a story. By regularly evaluating engagement, sentiment, conversions, ROI, and long-term impact, you can fine-tune your strategies, address issues before they become problems, and keep your brand on a path of sustainable growth.

4.3 Maximizing Reach: Leveraging User-Generated Content

The Power of User-Generated Content

In an age where authenticity is prized above all else, few tools are as valuable as user-generated content (UGC). At its core, UGC is content created by your customers, community members, or followers—whether through social media posts, product reviews, or video testimonials. This content is often seen as more credible than traditional advertising because it comes from real people rather than a brand. By leveraging UGC, brands can tap into a wellspring of authentic, relatable content that resonates deeply with their audience. It's a powerful tool for not just increasing reach but fostering trust, engagement, and long-term loyalty.

The beauty of user-generated content lies in its ability to humanize a brand. When potential customers see others like them interacting with a product or service, it feels more personal and less like a marketing ploy. UGC enables businesses to highlight their community, turning their audience into advocates and creating a sense of belonging. As consumers increasingly seek out brands that align with their values and lifestyles, UGC provides a window into how real people experience your products and services, creating a bridge between the brand and the consumer.

Cultivating a Culture of Sharing

To truly harness the power of UGC, brands must first foster a culture of sharing. This involves creating an environment where your audience feels comfortable contributing their thoughts, experiences, and creativity. One of the most effective ways to encourage this is by incentivizing participation. For example, running contests, challenges, or giveaways that ask your community to share photos, videos, or stories about your brand can spark a wave of content creation. When people feel like their contributions are valued, they're more likely to engage and share their experiences.

Another vital component of cultivating a culture of sharing is building a sense of community. Your audience needs to know that their voices are heard and appreciated. This can be achieved by engaging with user-generated content—liking, commenting, and resharing it to your social channels. When your followers see that you're actively interacting with their posts, they feel recognized, which increases the likelihood of future participation.

Amplifying Your Message through UGC

Once you've started to gather UGC, the next step is to amplify it. Sharing user-generated content across your marketing channels—whether on social media, your website, or email campaigns—extends the reach of both your message and your community's voice. When resharing content, always ensure that you give proper credit to the original creator. This not only acknowledges their contribution but also encourages others to participate, knowing they'll be recognized.

By incorporating UGC into paid advertisements or influencer campaigns, you take your marketing to the next level. UGC works especially well in paid social media ads, where audiences tend to tune out traditional, polished marketing content. Ads featuring real people using your products or services feel more authentic and less "salesy," which can drive better results. User-generated content also tends to have higher engagement rates, making it a key asset in boosting the effectiveness of your campaigns.

Moreover, showcasing UGC on your website or in product descriptions can help potential customers relate to your brand. A customer who is looking to buy may find comfort in seeing others enjoying the same product or service they are considering. Reviews, testimonials, and user-submitted photos act as social proof, which has been shown to influence buying decisions. It reassures potential customers that they're making a good choice, backed by the experiences of others.

Long-Term Benefits of UGC

The power of user-generated content isn't just about short-term engagement or reaching a larger audience—it's also about building long-term relationships. By consistently promoting and sharing UGC, you are fostering a deeper connection between your brand and your audience. People like to feel that they are part of something larger than themselves, and by celebrating their contributions, you turn them into lifelong supporters.

Over time, UGC can become a cornerstone of your brand's identity. It shows that you value your customers and their experiences, rather than simply pushing a product. This leads to stronger brand loyalty, a sense of community, and a growing base of advocates who willingly share your brand with their networks. In turn, this creates a cycle of organic growth, as more and more people see how real individuals interact with your brand and feel inspired to join in.

The Future of Content Marketing

In today's digital ecosystem, user-generated content is one of the most effective ways to increase brand visibility and strengthen your marketing efforts. By leveraging the power of your community's creativity and authentic voices, you can maximize your reach and create lasting relationships with your audience. As brands continue to seek ways to stand out in an increasingly crowded market, UGC offers a unique opportunity to connect with consumers on a deeper, more personal level. The future of content marketing is no longer about pushing products but about building relationships—relationships that are fostered through the voices and stories of the very people who love and support your brand.

4.4 The Role of Storytelling in Unified Campaigns

The Power of Narrative in Marketing

Storytelling is a powerful tool that has been at the heart of human communication for centuries. From ancient myths passed down through generations to the content we consume today, stories have a unique ability to captivate, engage, and connect. In the realm of modern marketing, storytelling has become an essential component in crafting unified campaigns that resonate with audiences. When integrated thoughtfully, a compelling narrative can transform a brand's message, imbuing it with meaning and creating lasting emotional connections with consumers.

In a world saturated with advertisements, consumers are more discerning than ever. They're not just looking for products or services—they're seeking brands that speak to their values, experiences, and aspirations. A well-told story can cut through the noise, engaging the audience on a deeper level and leaving a lasting impact. Whether it's a brand's journey, the story behind a product, or the impact a company has on its community, storytelling provides the perfect vehicle for communicating what a brand stands for and why it matters. In this sense, storytelling is no longer a luxury; it's a necessity in building a unified and authentic marketing strategy.

Crafting a Cohesive Brand Story

For storytelling to be effective, it must be cohesive and consistent across all platforms and campaigns. A unified campaign means that every piece of content—whether it's an Instagram post, a YouTube video, or a blog article—tells a part of the same larger story. Each touchpoint with your audience should reinforce the brand narrative, creating a seamless experience that feels both personal and powerful.

A cohesive brand story is more than just a marketing tool; it's a reflection of your brand's identity. It should resonate with the core values that your business represents and align with the interests and needs of your target audience. This means understanding your audience deeply and crafting a narrative that speaks to their hopes, challenges, and desires. When a brand's story is authentic, it builds trust, fostering a sense of connection that drives long-term loyalty.

Moreover, a unified story ensures that all elements of a marketing campaign work together toward a common goal. Every post, tweet, ad, or email contributes to a larger narrative, amplifying the brand's message and strengthening its presence. Rather than creating isolated pieces of content that stand alone, storytelling weaves each piece together into a dynamic whole. This interconnectedness maximizes the impact of each campaign, creating a sense of harmony and continuity that makes the brand experience feel more unified and deliberate.

Emotional Engagement and Brand Loyalty

One of the key benefits of storytelling is its ability to elicit an emotional response. Humans are wired to connect with stories—they bring abstract concepts to life, making them more relatable and memorable. Whether it's through humor, empathy, or inspiration, a well-crafted story can forge an emotional bond between a brand and its audience. This bond goes beyond the transactional nature of typical marketing; it taps into the human need for connection and belonging.

When a brand's story resonates with its audience, it creates a sense of shared experience. Consumers don't just buy products; they become part of the brand's narrative. They invest emotionally, forming an attachment that turns them into loyal advocates. This is particularly true in the digital age, where consumers are constantly interacting with brands across multiple touchpoints. A compelling story that connects emotionally can inspire consumers to not only choose your brand over competitors but also share that story with their networks. This word-of-mouth marketing, fueled by an emotionally engaged audience, can have a far-reaching impact.

Integrating Storytelling with Influencer Campaigns

One of the most effective ways to amplify a brand story is by integrating storytelling into influencer campaigns. Micro-influencers, in particular, offer a unique opportunity to tell authentic, relatable stories to a targeted audience. When influencers share personal stories about how they interact with your brand, it brings an additional layer of authenticity and relatability to the narrative.

Influencers already have the trust of their followers, making them powerful storytellers. By collaborating with influencers who align with your brand's values, you can amplify your message and create a broader, more engaged audience. This partnership allows you to extend your brand story beyond your immediate circle, tapping into new communities and networks while maintaining the authenticity and cohesion of your narrative.

The Lasting Impact of Storytelling

Storytelling is not just a technique to boost sales—it's a fundamental aspect of how brands connect with people. When integrated into a unified campaign, it turns marketing into a conversation, creating relationships that go beyond transactions. By telling a compelling, cohesive story that resonates with your audience, you not only differentiate your brand in a crowded marketplace but also create long-lasting emotional connections that drive loyalty. As brands continue to evolve, storytelling will remain at the heart of any successful marketing strategy, shaping how businesses engage, influence, and inspire their audiences.

Chapter 5: Sustaining Growth and Innovation

The Quest for Sustainable Growth

In the world of business, growth is often seen as the ultimate goal. Companies strive for success by increasing revenue, expanding their reach, and outpacing the competition. But as every entrepreneur knows, growth is not a linear process. It ebbs and flows, presenting new challenges and opportunities at every turn. The key to long-term success is not just in achieving growth but in sustaining it. Sustainable growth is a delicate balance, built on a foundation of continuous innovation, adaptability, and strategic foresight.

The desire for growth can sometimes lead companies to rush into new markets, products, or strategies. However, true sustainable growth requires a more thoughtful approach. It's about making the right decisions at the right time—decisions that not only expand the company's footprint but also create value for customers and stakeholders. It's a mindset that prioritizes long-term success over short-term wins. To sustain growth, companies must remain nimble, constantly reassessing their goals, strategies, and tactics to ensure they're always evolving with the market.

The Role of Innovation in Growth

Innovation is the lifeblood of any business aiming for sustained growth. It's not just about introducing new products or technologies—it's about fostering a culture of creativity and problem-solving that permeates every level of the organization. Innovation can come in many forms: from improving internal processes to reimagining customer experiences, to rethinking business models altogether.

In the digital age, innovation is no longer a luxury; it's a necessity. The rapid pace of technological advancement and shifting market demands mean that businesses must innovate or risk being left behind. Successful companies are those that anticipate trends and adapt quickly, continually reinvesting in research and development, and staying ahead of their competitors. But true innovation goes beyond just creating something new—it's about delivering value. Every new idea or product must solve a problem or meet an unmet need, which is what drives sustained growth.

Innovation is also about reinvention. Businesses must be willing to reevaluate their operations, embrace new technologies, and adopt fresh perspectives. A company that clings to outdated methods may find itself stuck in a rut, unable to capitalize on new opportunities. However, companies that embrace change, experiment with new ideas, and take calculated risks are those that can consistently outpace their competition and continue to grow.

Building a Culture of Continuous Improvement

One of the most important factors in sustaining growth is the establishment of a culture of continuous improvement. This requires fostering an environment where employees feel empowered to experiment, learn from failure, and contribute to the company's overall growth strategy. Innovation doesn't just come from top-down directives—it's often born from the creativity and insights of those on the front lines of the business.

In a company that values continuous improvement, feedback loops are essential. Employees, customers, and stakeholders all play a critical role in identifying areas for innovation and development. By actively listening to their insights and acting on their feedback, companies can create products and services that not only meet but exceed expectations. Furthermore, a culture of continuous improvement encourages employees to take ownership of their roles, leading to higher engagement and productivity. This, in turn, directly contributes to the company's ability to grow and innovate over time.

Staying Ahead of the Curve: Anticipating Future Trends

To truly sustain growth, businesses must become experts in forecasting future trends. The most successful companies are those that can anticipate shifts in consumer behavior, technology, and industry dynamics before they happen. This requires a deep understanding of the market, a commitment to research and development, and the ability to spot emerging opportunities early.

Rather than waiting for change to happen, innovative companies actively create it. They're constantly exploring new ways to disrupt the status quo, testing out novel ideas, and adapting their strategies accordingly. The ability to stay ahead of the curve is not just about being reactive—it's about being proactive and continuously shaping the future.

This forward-thinking approach requires a balance between risk and reward. While taking bold risks can lead to tremendous growth, it also requires the courage to fail and learn from mistakes. A culture that embraces experimentation and failure as learning experiences is essential to staying ahead of the curve. Businesses that fear failure will often miss out on opportunities to innovate, while those that take calculated risks with a focus on long-term growth are the ones that continue to thrive.

Sustaining growth and innovation is not a one-time effort; it's a journey that requires ongoing commitment and adaptation. Companies must constantly evolve, embracing new ideas, technologies, and strategies to meet the ever-changing demands of the marketplace. But at the heart of sustainable growth lies a simple truth: businesses that prioritize innovation, continuous improvement, and the ability to anticipate trends are the ones that will thrive in the long run.

By creating a culture that fosters creativity, staying agile in the face of change, and being proactive in shaping the future, businesses can build a foundation for lasting success. In an increasingly competitive and dynamic world, the key to sustained growth lies not just in how a company grows, but in how it continues to evolve, innovate, and adapt to the challenges and opportunities of the future.

5.1 Staying Ahead: Trends Shaping Online Engagement and Influencer Marketing

The Rapid Evolution of Digital Platforms

The landscape of online engagement and influencer marketing is constantly shifting. What works today may not work tomorrow, and the brands that succeed are those that can adapt to the ever-changing digital environment. One of the most significant trends shaping this space is the rapid evolution of digital platforms. Social media platforms like Instagram, TikTok, and YouTube have become the primary battleground for influencer marketing, but new players are constantly entering the scene, disrupting established norms.

For example, TikTok's rise has changed the way audiences consume content. Short, snackable videos have replaced long-form posts, making it easier for influencers to connect with their followers in authentic, spontaneous ways. Meanwhile, Instagram has embraced a more integrated approach, combining photos, stories, reels, and live broadcasts to keep users engaged throughout the day. Brands are increasingly recognizing the power of these platforms not just for advertising, but as a space for community-building and direct conversations with consumers.

To stay ahead in the influencer marketing game, brands must not only keep up with these changes but also anticipate them. It's no longer enough to simply target large audiences; marketers need to understand which platforms resonate with specific demographics and how to leverage the features of each platform to create meaningful content.

The Shift Toward Authenticity

Another critical trend that has emerged in recent years is the shift toward authenticity. Consumers, especially younger generations, have grown weary of overtly polished, inauthentic marketing. They crave genuine connections with brands and influencers that feel real and relatable. This has led to the rise of micro-influencers—individuals with smaller, more engaged followings who can offer personalized, authentic content.

In response to this demand, influencer marketing strategies are moving away from a focus on vanity metrics like follower count and moving toward engagement and relevance. Brands are looking for influencers who align with their values and can speak to their audiences in a meaningful way. This shift is empowering influencers to share more personal stories, build stronger connections with their followers, and, ultimately, foster more lasting brand loyalty.

As this trend continues to evolve, brands must refine their influencer marketing strategies to prioritize authenticity over the appearance of perfection. It's no longer about broadcasting a message; it's about starting a conversation and fostering genuine connections.

The Power of Data-Driven Decision Making

The integration of data analytics into influencer marketing is another trend that cannot be overlooked. As brands seek to maximize their ROI, they are increasingly turning to data-driven decision-making to measure the effectiveness of their campaigns. Influencers themselves are also leaning into analytics to understand what resonates with their audiences, refining their content to deliver even more value.

This trend has led to a greater focus on measurable metrics such as engagement rates, click-through rates, and conversion rates. It's not enough to simply track likes and shares; brands need to understand the impact of influencer collaborations on real business outcomes. Advanced tools now allow for deeper insights into consumer behavior, making it easier for marketers to track the performance of their campaigns and optimize them in real-time.

By embracing data, brands can make smarter decisions about which influencers to work with, what type of content to produce, and how to best reach their target audiences. This focus on data-driven marketing is not only making influencer campaigns more effective but also more transparent, helping to build trust between brands, influencers, and consumers.

Interactive Content and Community Engagement

Finally, interactive content is becoming a powerful tool for driving engagement. From polls and quizzes to user-generated content and live-streaming events, the shift towards more interactive forms of communication is transforming the influencer marketing landscape. Audiences want to feel involved and heard, and brands are responding by encouraging conversations rather than simply broadcasting messages.

Influencers are now engaging with their audiences in real time through live broadcasts, Q&A sessions, and product demonstrations, fostering a deeper sense of community and connection. By allowing followers to participate in the creation of content—whether through comments, shares, or co-created campaigns—brands can build a loyal, engaged community that feels like an integral part of their journey.

This trend is also reflected in the rise of user-generated content (UGC), where brands encourage their followers to share their own experiences with products. UGC not only amplifies brand messages but also helps build trust, as consumers are more likely to believe recommendations from their peers than from paid influencers.

Navigating the Future of Engagement

As the digital world continues to evolve, staying ahead of trends in online engagement and influencer marketing will require both agility and foresight. Brands must be prepared to adapt to new platforms, prioritize authenticity in their messaging, leverage data analytics to drive decisions and foster meaningful, interactive relationships with their audiences. The companies that thrive in the ever-changing digital landscape will be those that stay ahead of the curve, anticipate shifts in consumer behavior, and create lasting, impactful connections with their communities.

5.2 Scaling Without Losing Authenticity

The Dilemma of Growth

As brands scale their efforts, they often face the delicate challenge of growing their reach without sacrificing the authenticity that made them successful in the first place. In the fast-paced world of digital marketing and influencer collaborations, the urge to expand rapidly can be overwhelming. However, rapid growth can sometimes mean stepping away from the values and principles that resonate with a brand's core audience. For a brand to maintain its integrity and its connection with consumers, it must navigate the waters of scaling without losing the essence of what made it trustworthy and relatable in the first place.

This balancing act requires careful thought and intention, as authenticity cannot be manufactured. It is something that needs to be nurtured over time. Scaling without sacrificing authenticity is not about simply reaching more people; it's about maintaining the depth of connection with your existing audience while expanding that connection to a broader group.

Building a Scalable Foundation of Values

At the heart of maintaining authenticity during growth is a clear, consistent set of values that guide the brand's every move. The foundation of a brand's identity must be built on principles that resonate with both the brand's leadership and its audience. These values must be deeply woven into every aspect of the brand's operations, from the way it communicates with followers to the influencers it collaborates with.

When brands remain true to their values, it becomes easier to scale without losing the essence of what made them successful. The key is to stay focused on why you're growing in the first place. Are you expanding simply to make a profit, or are you doing so because you believe in something larger—such as providing value, solving a problem, or creating a community? By keeping these guiding principles in mind, you ensure that scaling doesn't come at the expense of authenticity.

For instance, a beauty brand that has built its reputation on eco-friendly products and ethical practices must continue to prioritize these values, even as it grows. As the company scales, it may be tempting to reduce costs or cut corners, but maintaining a commitment to sustainability can differentiate the brand in the marketplace and help it remain true to its original mission.

Fostering Genuine Influencer Relationships

Influencer partnerships are a powerful way to scale a brand's reach. However, as a brand grows, it's easy to lose the authenticity of these collaborations. The key to preserving authenticity in influencer marketing is to build genuine, long-term relationships with influencers who share your values, rather than focusing on quick, transactional partnerships.

Instead of simply seeking influencers with the largest followings, brands should prioritize creators whose audiences align with the brand's core demographic and whose values align with the brand's mission. Authentic influencer marketing is not about pushing products—it's about fostering a relationship built on trust, transparency, and mutual respect.

For example, rather than collaborating with influencers who have mass appeal, a brand might choose to work with micro-influencers who have smaller, but highly engaged audiences. These influencers tend to have a more personal relationship with their followers, making their recommendations feel more authentic and relatable. This kind of collaboration strengthens the brand's narrative and fosters loyalty among consumers.

Maintaining Personalization as You Expand

As a brand grows, personalization becomes increasingly difficult, but it remains essential for maintaining authentic connections. It's important to scale in a way that doesn't dilute the personal touch that made the brand special to its original audience. This can be achieved by leveraging technology in a way that enhances personal connections rather than replacing them.

For example, automated email marketing can still be personalized with dynamic content based on the recipient's preferences, behaviors, or past interactions. Similarly, chatbots or AI-driven customer service tools can be used to provide quick, helpful responses without sacrificing the human element of communication.

Personalization can also be incorporated into influencer partnerships. Instead of using the same message for all influencers, brands can work with their influencers to create unique, individualized content that speaks to different segments of their audience. This ensures that the message feels tailored, rather than generic, which helps maintain the authenticity of the brand's voice.

Growth Without Compromise

Scaling a brand without losing authenticity is not an impossible task, but it does require a commitment to values, relationships, and personalization. As a brand grows, it's essential to keep in mind what made it successful in the first place and ensure that growth is aligned with those core principles. By staying focused on authenticity—whether in values, influencer partnerships, or customer relationships—brands can successfully scale while deepening their connections with their audiences. The key is not just to grow, but to grow with purpose, maintaining the trust and loyalty that made your brand truly stand out.

5.3 The Long Game: Building Loyalty and Advocacy

The Foundation of Loyalty

In a world driven by instant gratification and fleeting trends, cultivating loyalty is not just a marketing strategy—it is an art form. While many businesses focus on short-term sales and quick returns, the true success of a brand lies in its ability to foster long-term relationships. Loyalty is born not out of a single transaction or a fleeting interaction, but through consistent, meaningful engagement that adds value to the customer's life. It's about creating experiences that resonate deeply and continuously, leaving a lasting impression long after the initial contact.

Building loyalty is a gradual process, one that requires businesses to be patient and invested in their customers' journey. It's about showing up authentically time and time again, offering something that makes people feel heard, understood, and valued. This is the foundation upon which advocacy is built—customers who believe in a brand enough to not only return but to actively champion it to others.

Nurturing Relationships Over Time

Loyalty is not something that happens overnight. It is cultivated through continuous interaction, where every touchpoint offers an opportunity to build trust. One of the most powerful tools in this process is personalized communication. Whether it's a tailored email, a special discount on a customer's birthday, or a response to a comment on social media, these gestures make customers feel like they matter beyond just being a source of revenue. In a world flooded with impersonal marketing tactics, authenticity and attention to detail are the rare gems that differentiate successful brands from those that struggle to retain their customers.

The key to this ongoing relationship is consistency. It's easy to lose sight of loyalty in pursuit of growth or new customer acquisition, but a brand that forgets its existing customers in favor of attracting new ones will soon find itself struggling to maintain its relevance. By ensuring that your most loyal customers feel valued at every stage of their journey, you cultivate a sense of community and inclusion that encourages them to return again and again.

Transforming Loyalty Into Advocacy

True brand advocacy comes when customers take it upon themselves to speak on your behalf when they feel so deeply connected to your brand that they actively recommend it to others. But this transformation from loyal customer to passionate advocate doesn't happen by accident. Advocacy is the natural result of consistently exceeding expectations and creating experiences so compelling that customers feel compelled to share them.

Creating advocates requires more than just delivering a great product or service—it demands an emotional connection. When customers feel that they are part of something larger, something they believe in, they become your most powerful marketers. This is why brands that focus on values, community, and social responsibility often see higher levels of advocacy. Customers who share your beliefs or resonate with your mission are more likely to become vocal supporters, spreading your message far beyond traditional marketing channels.

One of the most effective ways to build advocacy is through storytelling. Sharing the stories of how your brand has impacted real people helps customers connect on a deeper level. When they see themselves in those stories, they are more likely to feel emotionally invested in your brand's success. This is where the magic happens—the transition from a transactional relationship to one based on shared values, passions, and a sense of purpose.

The Ripple Effect of Advocacy

Once customers become advocates, their influence spreads in ways that far outstrip any paid advertisement. Their recommendations are seen as trustworthy and genuine, and they have the power to sway others in ways that traditional marketing simply cannot. Whether it's through word-of-mouth, social media shares, or product reviews, advocates act as an extension of your brand, amplifying your message to a wider audience.

To continue nurturing this advocacy, businesses must ensure that they continue delivering exceptional experiences and offering value. The relationship does not end once a customer has become an advocate—it requires ongoing attention and care. Brands that treat their advocates with the same level of respect and value as their most loyal customers ensure that these advocates remain invested in the brand for years to come.

A Brand's Legacy Built on Loyalty

In the end, the long game of building loyalty and advocacy is what sustains a brand over time. It's about creating a foundation that is rooted in trust, respect, and a genuine connection with customers. When brands focus on nurturing their relationships with existing customers and turning them into advocates, they create a ripple effect that extends beyond any advertising campaign. The result is a brand that not only survives but thrives, thanks to the unwavering support of customers who are passionate about its mission. Building loyalty and advocacy may take time, but the rewards are more than worth the effort, as it creates a legacy that outlasts trends and positions the brand as a trusted partner in the lives of its audience.

5.4 Creating a Roadmap for Future Success

Laying the Foundation for Long-Term Growth

Success is never an accident. It's a journey built on intentional actions, thoughtful planning, and an unwavering commitment to continuous improvement. While the future is inherently uncertain, having a roadmap allows businesses to navigate the complexities of change with clarity and purpose. A roadmap for future success isn't merely a plan—it's a strategic guide that empowers businesses to thrive, adapt, and evolve. It's a living document that grows with the business, providing the necessary framework for sustainable growth in the face of shifting markets and emerging opportunities.

Building a solid roadmap starts with a clear understanding of the business's core values, vision, and long-term goals. Without this foundational clarity, any effort to build for the future will be aimless. The vision should not just reflect where a company wants to be in five or ten years but also what it stands for—its purpose, its mission, and the impact it seeks to make. When businesses align their day-to-day decisions with a long-term vision, they create a sense of direction that keeps them on track through challenges, setbacks, and the inevitable shifts in the market landscape.

Setting Milestones and Defining Key Objectives

Once the foundation is established, the next step is to break the journey down into manageable milestones. These milestones act as signposts along the way, marking important achievements and helping businesses assess whether they are on the right path. Setting realistic, measurable objectives provides a clear sense of progress and motivates teams to stay focused on their goals.

However, it's important to recognize that success isn't always linear. As markets evolve and consumer behaviors shift, businesses must remain flexible enough to pivot when necessary. While a roadmap provides structure, it's the agility to adjust that ensures businesses can navigate the ever-changing business environment without losing momentum. The key is to remain open to new opportunities while staying true to the core mission.

Embracing Innovation as a Constant

No roadmap for success would be complete without acknowledging the power of innovation. In an age where technology and consumer expectations evolve at a rapid pace, the ability to innovate is no longer just a competitive advantage—it's essential for survival. Businesses must embed a culture of innovation into their roadmap, recognizing that creativity, problem-solving, and adaptability are integral to sustained success.

Innovation can take many forms. It might mean adopting new technologies that streamline operations, launching products that meet emerging customer needs, or exploring new marketing strategies that engage audiences in fresh ways. Businesses that fail to innovate risk falling behind, unable to keep up with competitors who are continuously evolving. This is why a roadmap for success must be fluid enough to incorporate innovation, allowing businesses to capitalize on opportunities before they pass.

Building a Strong Team for the Future

A company's greatest asset is its people. As businesses plan for the future, they must also consider how they will cultivate and maintain a talented workforce capable of executing the vision. Building a roadmap for success requires identifying the key roles and skills needed to drive the company forward. Investing in training, development, and team-building initiatives ensures that the business has the right people in place to tackle the challenges ahead.

Moreover, fostering a culture of collaboration, creativity, and empowerment is essential. A strong, motivated team that is aligned with the company's vision will be better equipped to execute the roadmap and bring future success to life. Businesses that fail to invest in their people often find themselves hindered by a lack of talent or motivation, unable to carry out the very strategies they have set in place.

Navigating Challenges and Celebrating Wins

Along the way, businesses will inevitably face challenges—economic downturns, competitive pressures, shifting consumer trends, and unforeseen obstacles. A well-crafted roadmap acknowledges these challenges and includes strategies for mitigating risks and overcoming adversity. This might mean diversifying revenue streams, finding new markets, or refining product offerings to stay relevant.

At the same time, it's essential to celebrate milestones and successes, no matter how small they may seem. Celebrating achievements, whether it's the successful launch of a new product or reaching a key financial target, reinforces the journey's purpose and motivates the team to keep pushing forward. Success is a result of continuous effort, and recognizing those efforts along the way creates a sense of accomplishment and shared purpose.

The roadmap for future success is not a static document. It evolves and adapts as the business progresses, reflecting new opportunities, challenges, and insights. By staying true to the core values and vision, setting clear milestones, embracing innovation, and investing in a strong team, businesses can build a future that is not only successful but sustainable. The roadmap isn't just a tool—it's the vehicle that drives businesses toward their highest potential. Success isn't about predicting the future, but about having the foresight and resilience to navigate it with confidence.

Conclusion:

In the ever-evolving landscape of online marketing, the power of community and the influence of micro-influencers has proven to be transformative forces. As businesses seek to rise above the noise of traditional marketing, the key to long-term success lies not in pushing products, but in building authentic relationships with an engaged and loyal audience. This book has explored the core principles of building online communities, leveraging the unique strengths of micro-influencers, and integrating these elements seamlessly into marketing strategies. Yet, the true challenge—and the true reward—comes in understanding how these elements work together to create a marketing ecosystem that nurtures growth, fosters trust, and cultivates brand loyalty.

The Heart of Engagement: Connection and Authenticity

At the heart of any thriving online community is a genuine sense of connection. As we've discussed, the strength of a community lies not in the size of the audience but in the depth of engagement. Communities that feel valued and understood are more likely to become passionate advocates for a brand. Building and nurturing these communities requires a commitment to authentic, consistent communication, as well as a deep understanding of what your audience truly cares about. From creating content that resonates to facilitating meaningful conversations, every interaction is an opportunity to strengthen the bond between a business and its followers.

When it comes to micro-influencers, this principle is no different. Their success comes not from their number of followers, but from their ability to authentically influence a niche audience. Micro-influencers have cultivated trust with their communities, and by collaborating with them, businesses gain access to an audience that values authenticity over flashy advertisements. The impact of such partnerships is profound—micro-influencers can inspire, educate, and persuade in ways that traditional marketing often cannot match.

Strategies for Sustainable Growth

To sustain long-term growth, businesses must embrace the ongoing process of learning, adapting, and evolving. The marketing landscape is dynamic, and to stay ahead, it's crucial to be agile—constantly refining strategies, exploring new opportunities, and responding to emerging trends. Building a roadmap for future success, as explored in Chapter 5, allows businesses to align their goals with the realities of the market while staying true to their core mission and values.

The future of online marketing lies in a seamless integration of community engagement and influencer collaborations. As businesses scale, they must be mindful of maintaining the authenticity that initially drew people in. Successful campaigns will continue to prioritize meaningful relationships, both with their community members and influencers. This combination of strategy, connection, and innovation will empower businesses to not only meet the demands of today's consumers but also anticipate and lead tomorrow's trends.

As you close this book, consider this a call to action. The strategies and insights shared here are not just theoretical; they are actionable tools that can be implemented today. Whether you are just beginning to explore the power of online communities or looking to refine your approach to influencer marketing, the possibilities are vast. The most successful businesses will be those that build communities that feel truly connected and collaborate with micro-influencers who share their values.

This is more than just a marketing strategy—it's a movement towards a new kind of business model, one built on trust, authenticity, and engagement. As you embark on your journey, remember that every step you take towards building meaningful connections, nurturing relationships, and collaborating with influencers is a step toward long-term success. The future of online marketing is in your hands—embrace it, and build something that will resonate for years to come.

In the end, it's not about the size of your audience or the number of your followers. It's about the depth of your connection, the authenticity of your message, and the power of the communities and influencers you bring together. That's where true business growth begins.